CONTENTS

INTRODUCTION

Welcome to *Metal Bass Lines*. I hope you enjoy learning these techniques.

ACCESSING THE AUDIO

To access the accompanying audio, go to **www.halleonard.com/mylibrary** and enter the code found on the first page of this book. This will grant you instant access to every example. Examples with accompanying audio are marked with an audio icon.

METAL TUNINGS

There are two tuning types that are common in metal: *standard tuning* and *drop tuning*. *Standard tuning* is when your bass is tuned in fourths (E-A-D-G). *Drop tuning* is when your lowest two strings are tuned a fifth apart, often with the low string tuned to D, then in fourths from there (D-A-D-G). Both tuning systems can be brought lower and higher in pitch.

Several exercises in this book are in drop tuning.

CHOP BUILDING AND PRACTICING

To begin, I would like to discuss some practice strategies that will help you build your chops. It's important to divide your practice time to address different areas of technique and musicianship.

First, let's look at why we practice. We practice for performance reasons. It might be for an upcoming show or recording session. That is a short-term goal. We also practice to keep improving as musicians and bassists. This is long-term reasoning. Sometimes, the two meet as you prepare for a single event.

When we play music or practice, there are three levels of thinking happening simultaneously: automatic, veiled, and controlled.

1. An *automatic* thinking process is when you are not aware of thinking or paying attention to what you are doing, but you are doing it.

2. A *veiled* thinking process means doing two things at the same time where one requires a little more attention and requires more control.

3. A *controlled* thinking process means doing something that requires all of your attention, where you focus your attention to control a specific task.

We need to incorporate all of these three levels of thinking into our practice because we are performing a number of different tasks at the same time. All of these tasks cannot have our full attention. Ask yourself, what requires your immediate attention when you are playing a piece of music? Is it the fingerings, the rhythm, and the form? The item that needs your full attention is the controlled process, the secondary task is veiled, and the one you are not even thinking about is the automatic process. You want to get to the point where you are paying attention to what is going on around you and interacting with the musicians in the band—where you are not worried about fingerings or the rhythm but you can make music and enjoy it. This is when you know your practicing has paid off!

We process music through three different memory systems: hearing it (aural), seeing it (visual), and feeling it (tactile). It's important to include all of these memory systems when you practice. This will help keep you from forgetting things because if one system fails, you can rely upon the others. If you practice scales frequently without reading them, you are only building a strong tactile memory. Taking another approach, if you really listen while you're playing, then you are also working on your aural system. Reading music and tabs or looking at your fingerboard while you play is building your visual memory system. Whatever your strength may be, you need to develop all of your memory systems and thinking processes on your instrument. I know of great musicians who practice scales while watching television. These are clues as to what kind of processing these musicians have accomplished through practicing.

Maintenance vs. Self-Improvement Practice

When I listen to different musicians practice, I find that there are two opposite ends of a spectrum. There is a level of practicing where you simply play things you like; mostly, music you can already play. This becomes a get-better-at-all-of-the-things-you-can-do kind of practicing. I call this *maintenance practice*. This is where you are really enjoying playing your instrument and making sure that you are keeping up your technique and repertoire.

Then, there is a practice of playing music and technical exercises that you cannot perform that is *self-improvement practice*. This kind of practice usually involves playing in awkward keys or tempos that are too fast or too slow, or simply things you can't do. This kind of practice is very tiring and can create a good amount of tension. Too much of this kind of practice could create physical problems with your playing.

Make sure that you blend these different kinds of practice into each session.

REHEARSING

Each practice session should contain both kinds of practicing and employ an *elaborative rehearsal method*. This technique of rehearsal involves making associations to other information you already know. By elaborating or creating a network of knowledge, you can create a deeper or richer understanding of the music on different levels. Most of us get locked into a *rote rehearsal method* at an early age. This technique is simply repeating the material over and over again to try to remember it. A common example used to illustrate this concept is repeating a phone number over and over again while running to the phone. It may last in your memory for a little while but it is soon forgotten. Sometimes this technique is confused with learning something by ear. If you learn something by ear and analyze it as a scale or arpeggio, then this is an elaborative rehearsal technique. If you just repeat it over and over again without trying to make a different connection each time, then you are learning by rote. Have you ever been playing a piece and you forget the music? It has happened to me on a number of occasions. If you need to go all the way back to the beginning of the piece to start again, you are not practicing properly and may be employing more of a rote rehearsal method.

PRACTICE PLANS

Ideally, if you really know a piece of music with your metal band, your thinking processes would look something like the table below.

AUTOMATIC	VEILED	CONTROLLED
Fingerings on Fretted Hand	Hooking Up with Others	Communicating/Band
Plucking Hand Patterns	Dynamics	Visual Cues
Pulse of the Tune	Articulation	Stage Presence
Aural Sense of Time/Form	Time Changes	Communicating/Audience

Now if you do not know the piece, the table would look something like the following table. Notice that there is no room for a number of items. Your short-term memory (controlled processes) has room for doing about seven things at once (stretching it). If you try more than that, you crash.

AUTOMATIC	VEILED	CONTROLLED
		Fingerings
		Plucked Hand Patterns
		Pulse
		Time/Form
		Time/Changes

This should start giving you the idea that you need to practice certain items to make them automatic and veiled, so you can pay attention to what is going on around you. Here is a blank table that you may copy and then use to monitor your practice or how well you know a piece.

AUTOMATIC	VEILED	CONTROLLED

Let's put this all together. You have heard of musicians practicing four-to-six hours a day. This is only productive if you take breaks in between and employ different kinds of practice. But I would like to suggest a weekly practice schedule based upon daily hour-long sessions, and you can modify this schedule to suit your specific needs. No matter what style of music you play, you should practice your technique, sound, and repertoire. And don't forget to include a 10-minute warm-up.

I like to practice in six-day cycles where I give myself a day off. This provides me with an incubation period where I can reflect on the music I am playing and look at things differently. On this "day off," I usually end up practicing without my instrument, which is another kind of elaborative rehearsal technique. The following routine emphasizes an elaborative rehearsal method putting all of the memory systems to use.

WEEK	10 MINUTES	15 MINUTES	5 MINUTES	30 MINUTES
Day 1	Warm up*	Exercise from Chapter*	Analyze form of song without your instrument	Try sight reading through song
Day 2	Warm up	Exercise from Chapter	Practice rhythm of song without instrument	Work on connections between scale and chord materials in the piece
Day 3	Warm up	Exercise from Chapter	Analyze song harmonic content and fingerings	Spot practice sections of song
Day 4	Warm up	Exercise from Chapter	Practice song without instrument	See how much you can play by ear
Day 5	Warm up	Exercise from Chapter	Practice difficult passages without instrument	Work on special sections with instrument
Day 6	Warm up	Exercise from Chapter	Sing song without instrument	Try to play song from memory

*All of the chapter examples could be used as warm-ups or exercises for building technique. Choose them accordingly to balance your technique.

This practice routine is based upon self-improvement and does not include maintenance practice, or just playing. It is quite rigorous, and you should blend both types of practice each day.

You should enjoy practicing. Practicing is a solitary event and should be blended with making music with others. Music is a social art, and if you are spending numerous hours in the practice room without playing with others, something is missing.

THE SOUND IS IN YOUR HANDS

Try practicing the electric bass without an amp. This can make you pay more attention to how your hands are actually producing the sound. It helps create a pallet of sound with your hands. Then, use the amp to color the sound. Try setting the amp EQ flat (all knobs at 12 o'clock); then, adjust it accordingly to fit the band.

Now, let's dive into some metal bass lines!

Early Metal Riffs

THE RIFF

In the late '60s and early '70s, bands such as Black Sabbath, Led Zeppelin, and Deep Purple defined the metal genre. Their music stemmed from the blues. In the blues, there is a basic form that includes a *riff*—a repetitive melodic figure, or "motif," usually two to four measures long. Riffs are often transposed to different pitch levels.

Here are some blues riffs typical of early metal. First, this two-bar riff is repeated, to become a four-bar phrase. It is based on a descending blues pentatonic scale.

FIG. 1.1. Four-Bar Riff

This four-bar riff is in a question-and-answer or "antecedent/consequent" phrase.

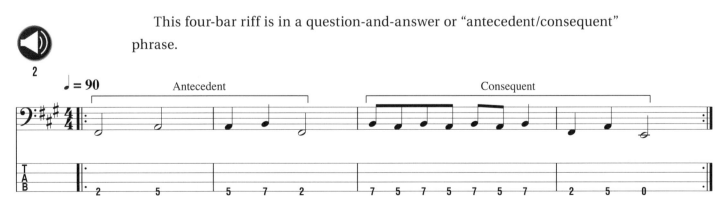

FIG. 1.2. Four-Bar Antecedent/Consequent Phrase

Here is a four-bar driving riff.

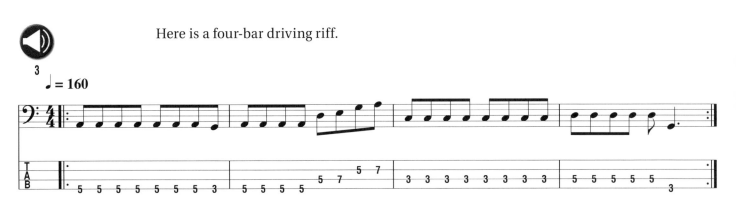

FIG. 1.3. Four-Bar Driving Riff

Here you see a two-bar riff sequence, transposing up a fourth.

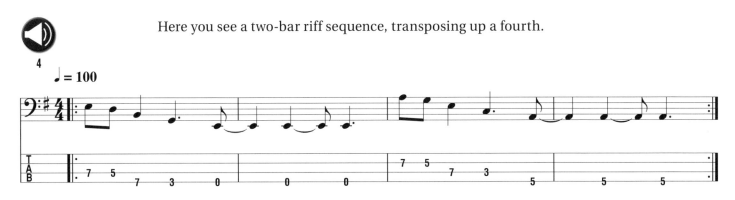

FIG. 1.4. Sequencing Riff

This next riff emphasizes the tritone, which is the flat-5 blue note.

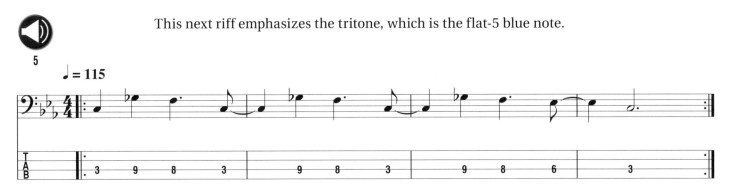

FIG. 1.5. Blue-Note Riff

Here is another antecedent and consequent four-bar phrase using E minor pentatonic.

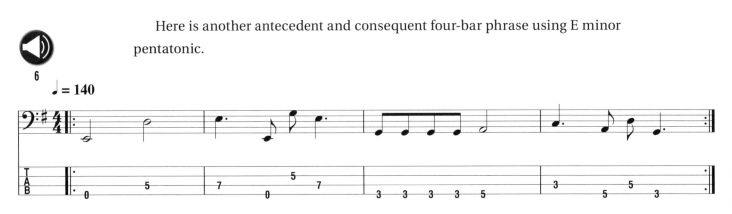

FIG. 1.6. E Minor Pentatonic Antecedent/Consequent Phrase

WRITE YOUR OWN

Write your own riff in the space below. Even if you just write in the tab, it's good practice to be able to document your riffs. It will give you more perspective on your bass lines.

First, write a two-bar riff.

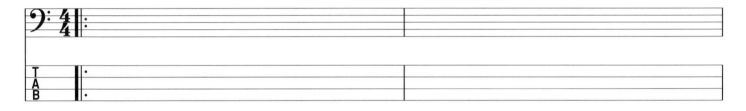

FIG. 1.7. Two-Bar Riff

Next, write a four-bar riff.

FIG. 1.8. Four-Bar Riff

Finally, write a four-bar riff that is organized as an antecedent and consequent phrase.

FIG. 1.9. Antecedent/Consequent Style Riff

ETUDE: THE SCRAPYARD

7: Full Band
8: Just Drums
9: No Bass

This song is composed of question-and-answer phrases. If it's difficult for you
to read, just listen and play along with the tablature.

David Marvuglio

FIG. 1.10. The Scrapyard

Multi-Finger Plucking Techniques

There are many ways to play time, from using a pick to multiple finger techniques. In this lesson, we are going to explore plucking techniques using your index, middle, and ring fingers. When practiced diligently, these techniques will allow you to play proficiently at faster speeds and with longer stamina.

I'm a right-handed bass player, so in this book, I refer to my right hand as the plucking/picking hand. Whatever hand you use to pluck the strings is the hand that plays time in metal.

First, try playing these exercises with two fingers. Then, try them with the three finger combinations listed below. Compare the sound and feeling of all combinations.

The first multi-finger combination (3-2-1) is used by players such as Alex Webster. This finger combination can be tricky at first when playing sixteenth notes because you have to learn to emphasize the downbeat with each finger.

The second combination (1-2-3-2) is used by players such as Steve Bailey. This combination allows the downbeat to be always played with your first finger in a four-note pattern.

The third combination (3-2-1-2) is used by players such as Steve DiGiorgio. It is similar to 1-2-3-2, except now, the ring finger emphasizes the downbeat.

The last multi-finger combination (1-3-2), which is what I primarily use, is similar to the Alex Webster combination except that you're starting on the first finger. I find that this allows making the transition into the triplet and galloping rhythms easier.

Experiment with each combination, and see what feels most comfortable for you. I use all of these combinations depending upon the different musical phrasing.

MULTI-FINGER PLUCKING COMBINATIONS

This series of exercises will help you choose the multi-fingering combination that is most comfortable for you. First, try all four fingering combinations shown.

FIG. **2.1.** Multi-Finger Plucking Exercise 1

Next, in figures 2.2 and 2.3, play the exercises using the most comfortable finger combination that you found in the previous example.

FIG. **2.2.** Multi-Finger Plucking Exercise 2

FIG. **2.3.** Multi-Finger Plucking Exercise 3

When playing eighth notes in this next exercise, use a two-finger plucking technique. For the sixteenths, use a multi-finger technique. This will help you transition between both techniques.

13

FIG. 2.4. Two- and Multi-Finger Plucking Technique Exercise

MOTOR PICKING VS. RAKING

Motor picking is a style where you keep your right hand sequence consistent, even when changing strings. This creates a consistent tone, especially for driving bass lines, since you are able to always strike through the string. This technique works with plucking and picking.

Raking is a technique where you draw your hand across two or more strings. This involves pulling on the strings while utilizing a plucking or picking technique. It has less driving and adds more finesse or detail to your pattern.

Try the next exercises using both techniques.

14

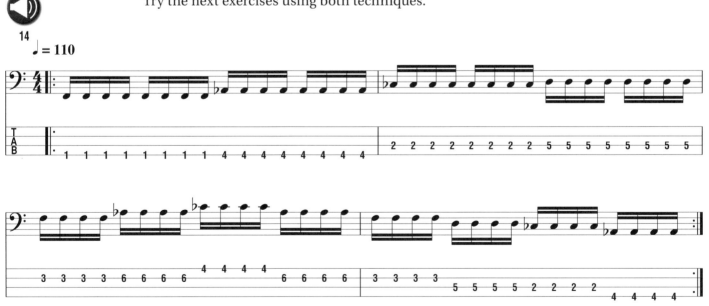

FIG. 2.5. Motor Picking and Raking Exercise

This next example is driving triplets. I find it most comfortable doing the 1-3-2 multi-finger sequence.

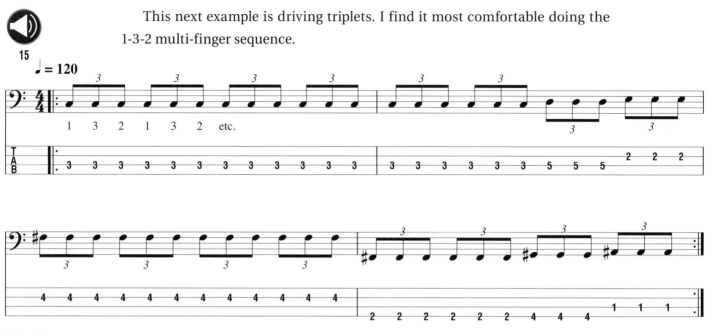

FIG. 2.6. 1-3-2 Multi-Fingered Sequence

WRITE YOUR OWN

Write your own fingering/picking sequence in the space below. Try to compose lines that require various string crossings and switching between different rhythms.

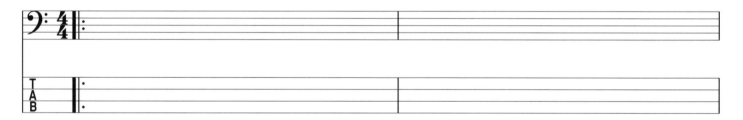

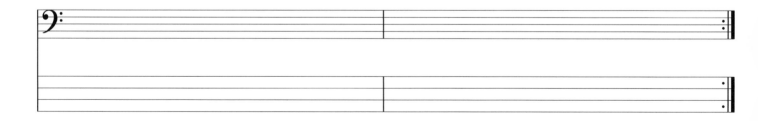

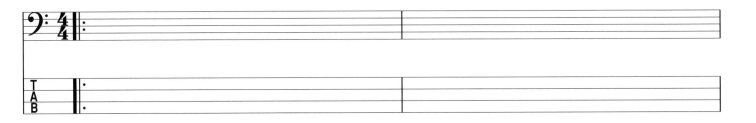

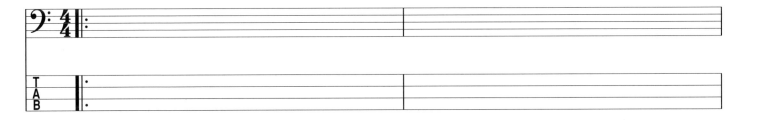

FIG. 2.7. Write Your Own Picking/Fingering

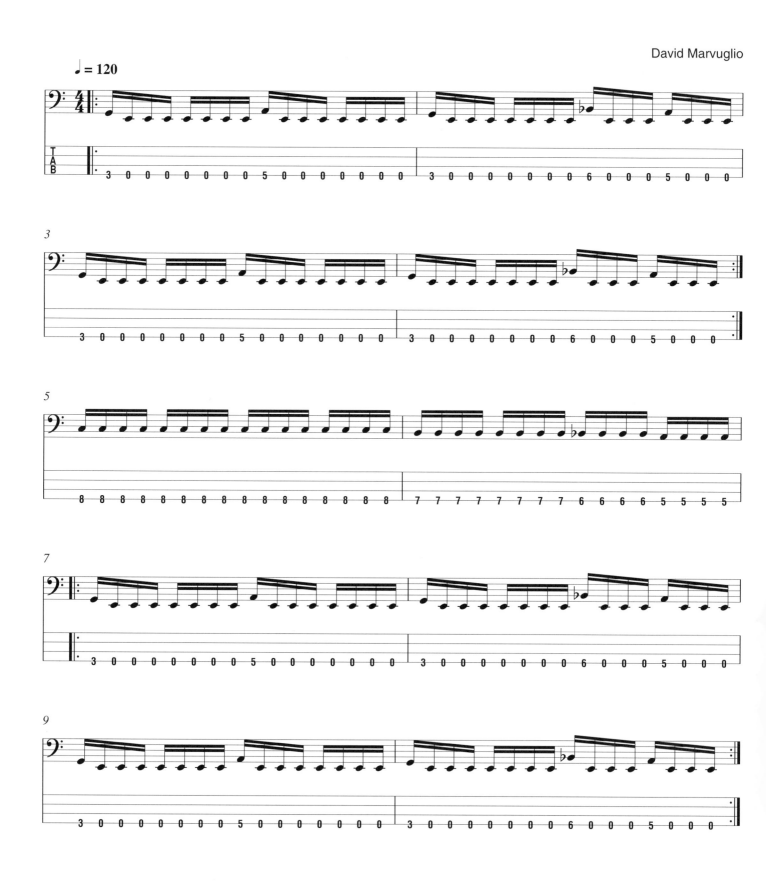

ETUDE: SKINLESS FINGERS

16: Full Band
17: Just Drums
18: No Bass

David Marvuglio

11

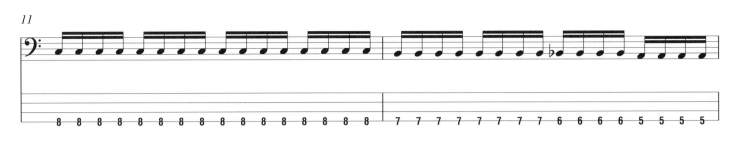

13

15

17

19

21

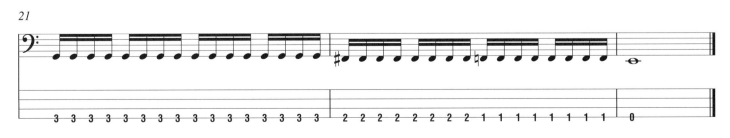

FIG. 2.8. Skinless Fingers

LESSON 3

Galloping Bass Lines

A *galloping bass line* is a driving bass line (see chapter 4) that consists of an eighth note followed by two sixteenth notes. These bass lines may appear in duple and triple meters. They come from a classical tradition and were made popular in metal by Steve Harris from Iron Maiden.

When practicing these exercises, keep an even rhythm and consistent tone. Pay particular attention to your picking or plucking patterns.

Here is the standard galloping rhythm with different picking and plucking configurations for the right hand.

19

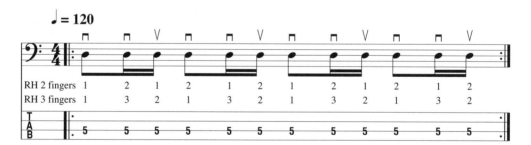

FIG. 3.1. Standard Galloping Rhythm

The next example is the rhythmic retrograde of the gallop. Notice the alterations for the right-hand picking pattern: ⊓ for a down stroke, and ∨ for an up stroke.

20

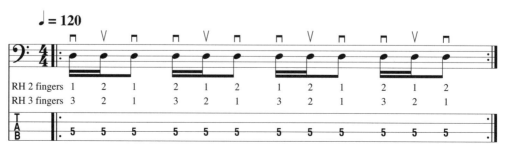

FIG. 3.2. Gallop Rhythm Retrograde

Figure 3.3 is the standard gallop with eighth-note approaches. Pay particular attention to your plucking/picking hand when crossing between the E and A strings.

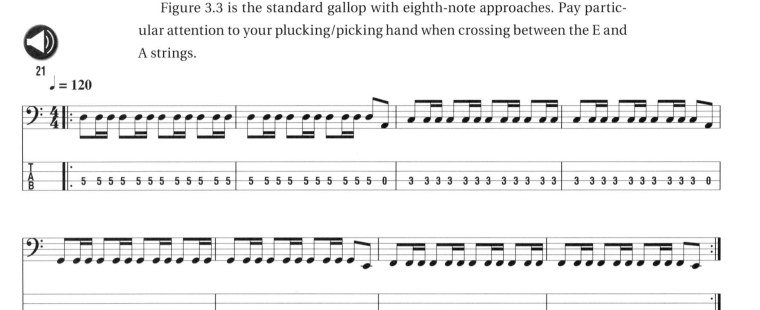

FIG. 3.3. Gallop with Eighth-Note Approaches

Figure 3.4 is a variation on the basic galloping pattern with an octave displacement and eighth-note syncopation.

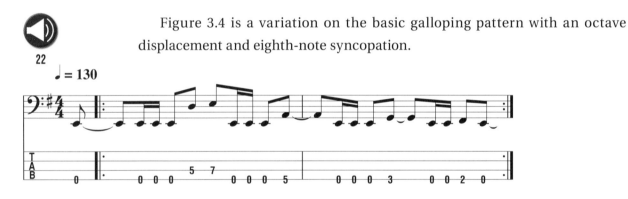

FIG. 3.4. Galloping with Octave Displacement

Here are a few exercises around galloping bass lines, which will help extend your technique and give you some ideas for variations of galloping bass lines. Begin at a tempo where you can play the exercise evenly, at a steady tempo, and with a good sound.

Figure 3.5 is a rhythmic retrograde gallop with the second sixteenth note acting as an anticipation to the eighth note. This creates a challenge of keeping the bass line even and not getting turned around.

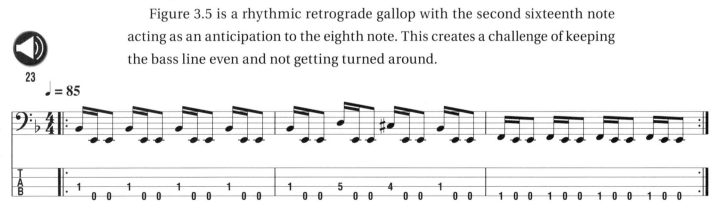

FIG. 3.5. Retrograde Gallop with Sixteenth Anticipation

Figure 3.6 is a rhythmic retrograde gallop with a sixteenth-note fill. Try to create your own two-beat sixteenth-note fills to connect the chords.

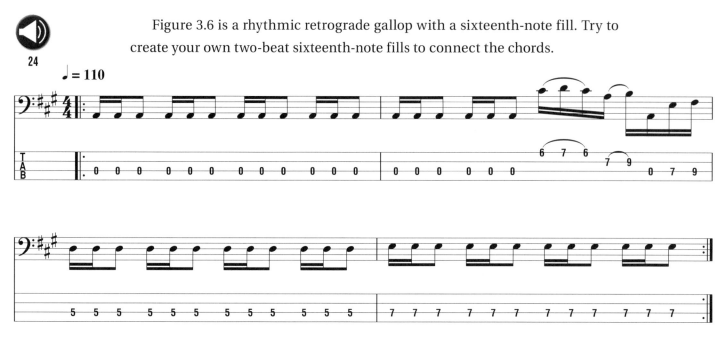

FIG. 3.6. Retrograde Gallop with Sixteenth-Note Fill

Figure 3.7 is a variation on the basic galloping pattern with an octave displacement. Note that this bass line is in 3/4 time and in drop-D tuning, where the lowest string is tuned down to D. (See the "Introduction" for more about drop tuning.)

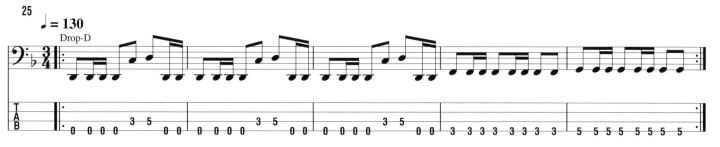

FIG. 3.7. Gallop Pattern with Octave Displacement

Figure 3.8 is using the rhythmic retrograde and traditional gallop with sustained arpeggios. This is a slightly more modern approach to the galloping bass line. It is similar to a Bach partita technique of creating compound melodic lines. Watch your rhythm switching between the two galloping rhythms.

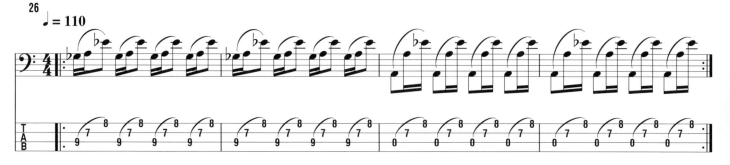

FIG. 3.8. Retrograde Gallop with Sustained Arpeggios

WRITE YOUR OWN

Write your own gallop rhythm in the space below.

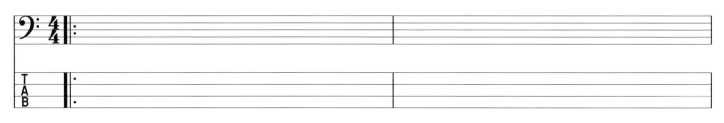

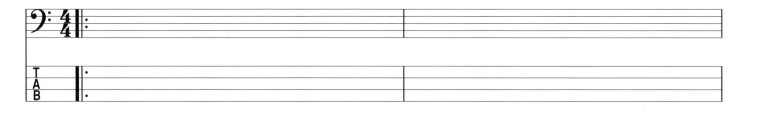

FIG. 3.9. Write Your Own Gallop

ETUDE: NEED FOR STEED (SADDLE UP)

27: Full Band
28: Just Drums
29: No Bass

Practice this etude using the following strategies, which will help you to learn any music:

- Before you play the etude at tempo, practice at whatever speed you can play it evenly. Then, increase the tempo gradually to bring it up to speed. Use a metronome.

- In addition to playing it at tempo, practice it at half time, and focus on tone consistency and right-hand technique.

- See how fast you can play it evenly. Work beyond the tempo of the track.

David Marvuglio

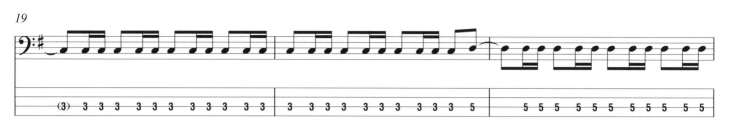

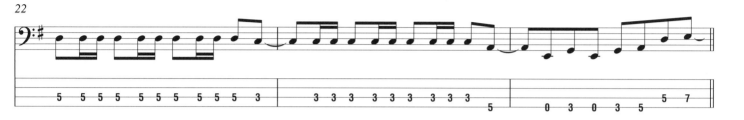

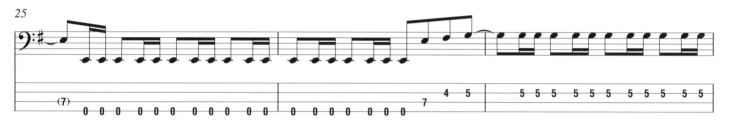

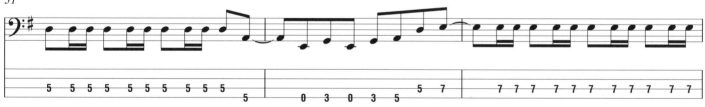

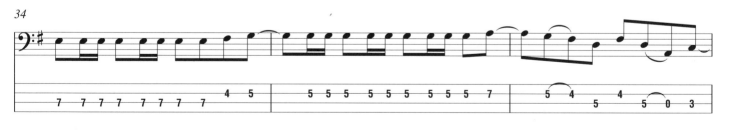

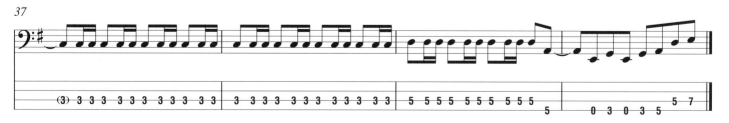

FIG. 3.10. Need for Steed (Saddle Up)

Driving Bass Lines

Driving bass lines are the essence of metal bass playing. This is what makes the listener want to bang their head and mosh.

A *driving bass line* has a repetitive rhythmic pattern, focusing on consistent eighth, triplet, or sixteenth rhythms. Many times, there are combinations of these rhythms to create a rhythmic pattern, which can also include rests. The bass player pumps it out, driving the beat and leading the band.

30   ♩ = 130

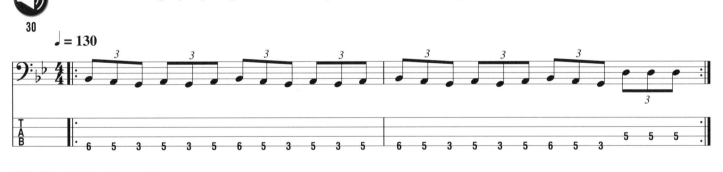

FIG. 4.1. Driving Bass Line

The following exercises will help you manage the band by driving the beat. Have fun playing along with the tracks.

EXERCISES

Figure 4.2 uses drop-D tuning. Tune your low E down to D; the other strings stay the same.

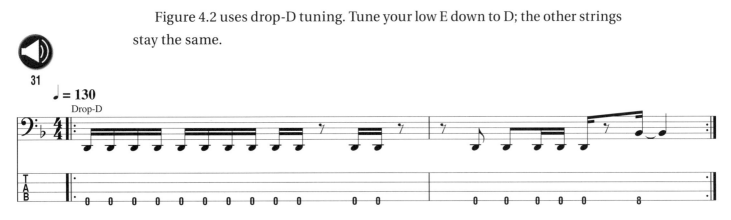

FIG. 4.2. Driving Bass Line Exercise 1

FIG. 4.3. Driving Bass Line Exercise 2

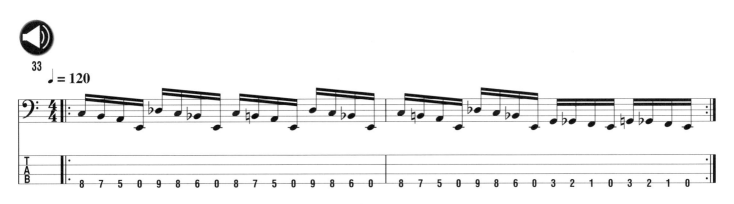

FIG. 4.4. Driving Bass Line Exercise 3

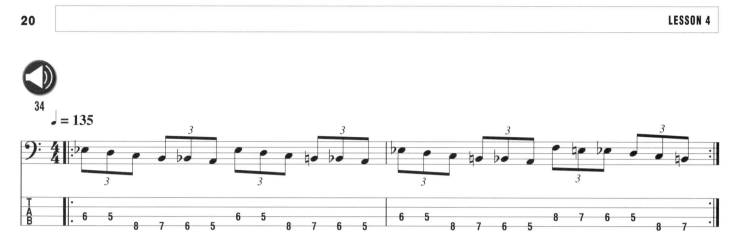

FIG. 4.5. Driving Bass Line Exercise 4

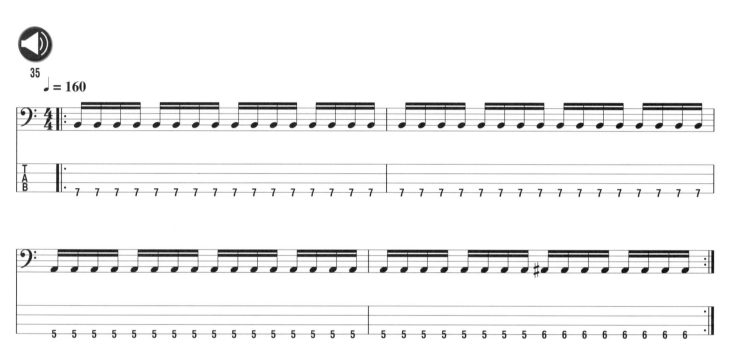

FIG. 4.6. Driving Bass Line Exercise 5

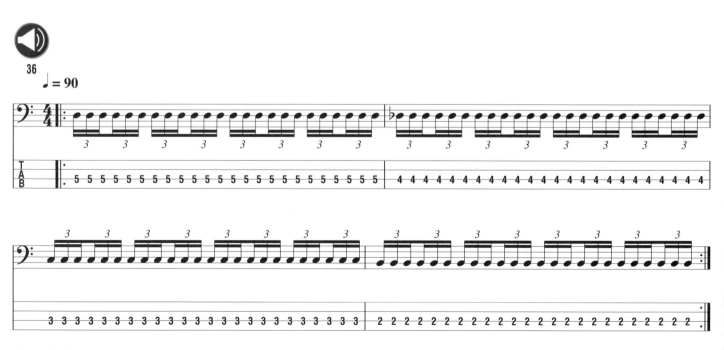

FIG. 4.7. Driving Bass Line Exercise 6

WRITE YOUR OWN

Write your own driving bass line in the space below. Try to compose some using eighths, triplets, sixteenths, and rests. Make sure it makes you want to bang your head when you are playing!

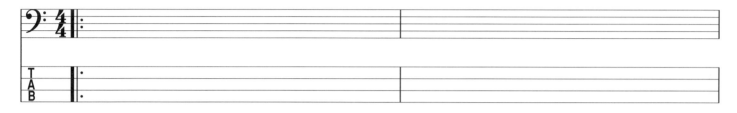

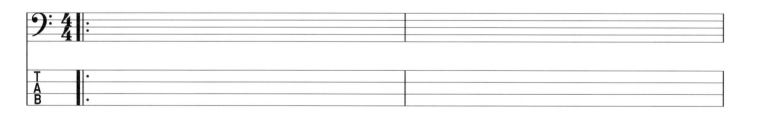

FIG. 4.8. Write Your Own Driving Bass Line

ETUDE: PANTHER HAMMER

37: Full Band
38: Just Drums
39: No Bass

David Marvuglio

$\quad$ = 110

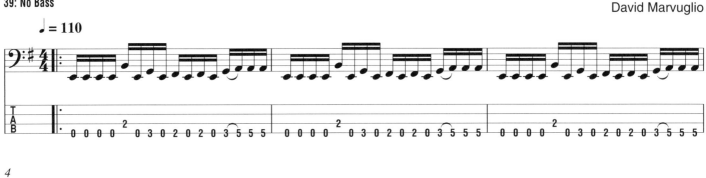

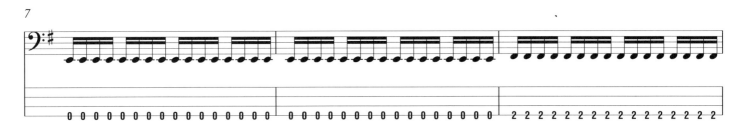

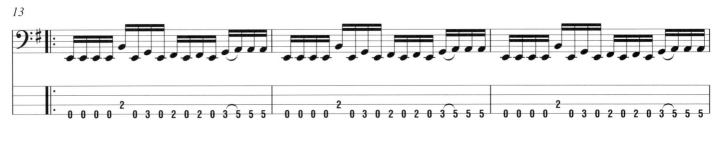

19

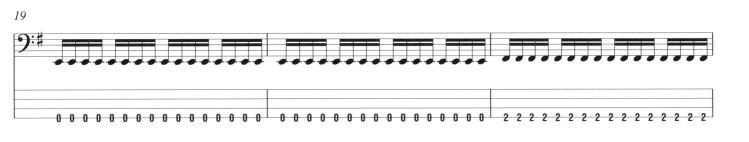

22

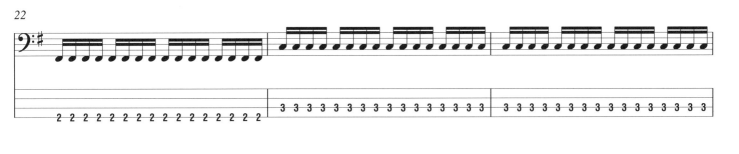

25

FIG. 4.9. Panther Hammer

Pedal Points and Double Stops

A *pedal point* is a note, usually the tonic (root) or 5 of the key, played continuously while notes from other chords play against it, often creating dissonance. In metal, this creates a static feel within the band, creating a "mantra" kind of groove. The following pedal-point bass lines combine the sustained tonic with elements from the progression.

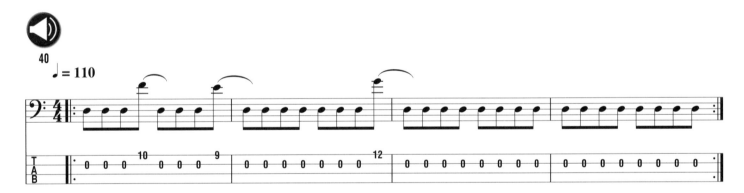

FIG. 5.1. Pedal Point Bass Line 1

FIG. 5.2. Pedal Point Bass Line 2

The next examples are pedal point lines that also include double and triple stops (chords) in the rhythmic groove.

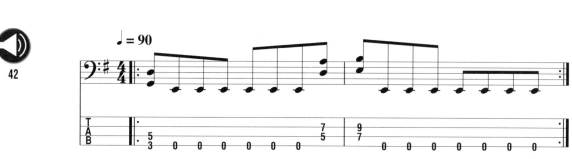

FIG. 5.3. Pedal Point with Double Stops

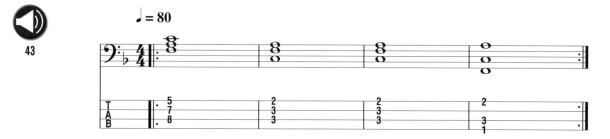

FIG. 5.4. Pedal Point (A) within Triple Stops

WRITE YOUR OWN

Write your own pedal point in the space below. Try writing the bass lines in
different keys. Experiment with double and triple stops.

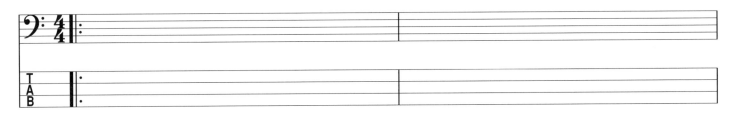

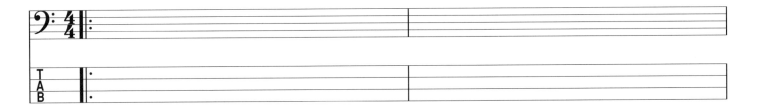

FIG. 5.5. Write Your Own Pedal Point Bass Line

ETUDE: WRENCH

44: **Full Band**
45: **Just Drums**
46: **No Bass**

David Marvuglio

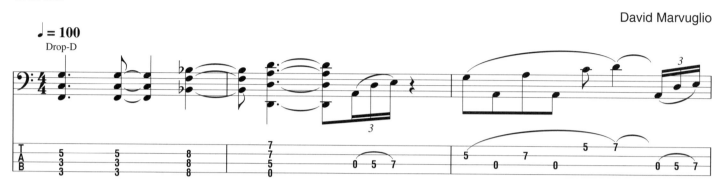

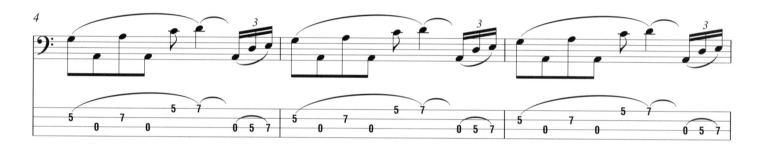

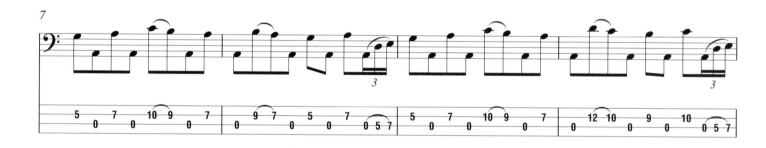

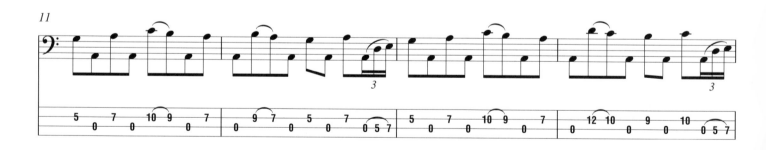

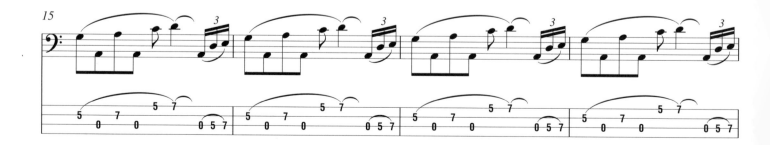

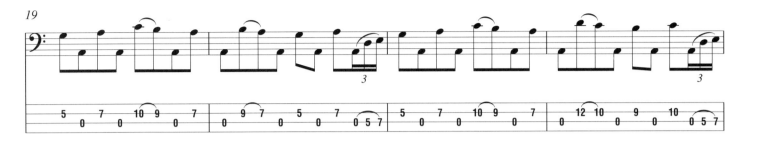

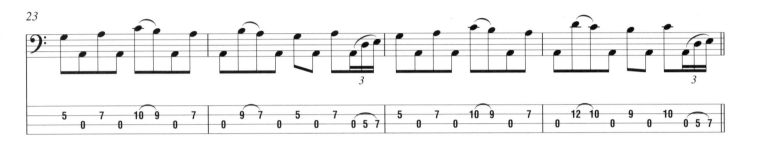

Repeat and fade out

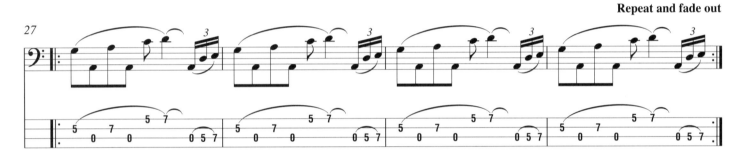

FIG. 5.6. Wrench

Tapping and Slapping Techniques

Tapping and slapping techniques involve both hands working to create different types of rhythmic and harmonic combinations. You can tap and slap with both hands. *Tapping* is fretting with either hand—usually a combination of both hands. It is similar to playing a piano on the fretboard. *Slapping* is striking the strings in a number of ways. The most common way is using your thumb of the plucking hand.

NAME	NOTATION	TECHNIQUE
Thumb	T	Use your thumb to strike the string against the fingerboard. This is the most common articulation in slap bass. It replaces the usual fingering of notes.
Thumb Up	U	Use your thumb to pull the string away from the fingerboard.
Dead Note	×	Mute the string so that it doesn't ring. This can be combined with other techniques. For example, using a T on a dead note is a good way to get an unpitched percussive sound.
Pop	P	Use your first or second finger of your right hand to pull up on the string. This is another one of the most common slap techniques. It is often used on high notes, and alternated with Ts.
Pull-Off		Use your left-hand fingers to articulate the notes by releasing the string. (Always high to low.)
Hammer-On		Use your left-hand fingers to articulate the notes by hitting the string against the fingerboard. (Always low to high.)
Slide		While the first note rings, slide up the fingerboard to the target note.
Left-Hand Slap	× L	Use your left-hand fingers to strike the strings against the fingerboard in a percussive manner. This is usually used with dead notes, muting the strings with your first finger and striking the notes with the others.

FIG. 6.1. Common Slap Articulations

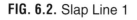

The next two examples require slapping with both hands. Now, we are going to play the bass like a percussion instrument. Play it slowly at first, and then bring it up to tempo.

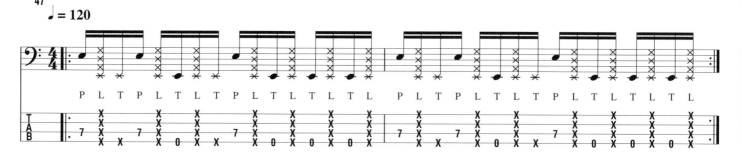

FIG. 6.2. Slap Line 1

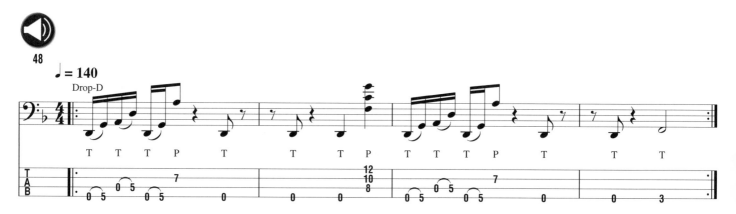

FIG. 6.3. Slap Line 2

This next example uses a double-thumb technique. Double thumbing is when you treat your thumb like a pick and use down and up strokes. This allows for greater speed than only down strokes, which is more common with the thumb.

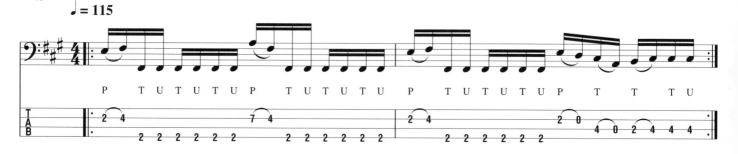

FIG. 6.4. Double-Thumb Technique

Here, we play the bass like a piano by using both hands to tap on the finger-board. In tap notation, L and R indicate the hand sounding the string; they are followed by fingering numbers (1 for first finger, 2 for second finger, etc.).

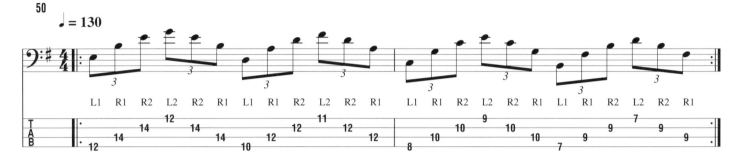

FIG. 6.5. Tapping the Fingerboard

This next example uses a tapping technique on one string. By using a combination of taps, hammer-ons, and pull-offs to execute arpeggios, we create a violin-like effect similar to what you hear in classical music, such as in Paganini and Bach.

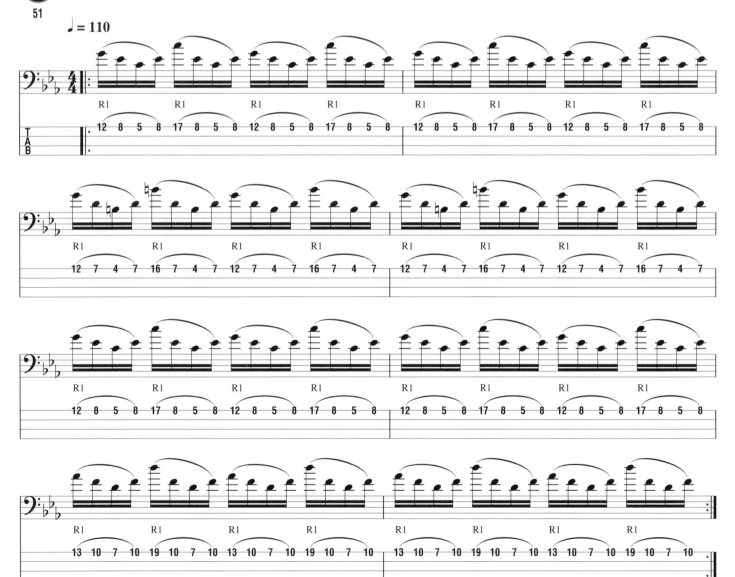

FIG. 6.6. Tapping on One String

This next example is like keeping the sostenuto pedal down on the piano. You accomplish this by holding down the chord with your fretting hand while playing a combination of taps and pull-offs with the plucking hand.

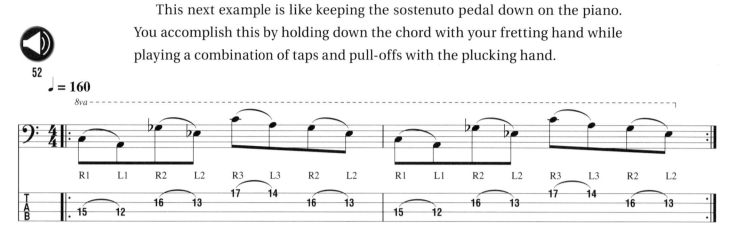

FIG. 6.7. Taps and Pull-Offs

WRITE YOUR OWN

Write your own four-bar phrases using slap and tapping techniques in the space below.

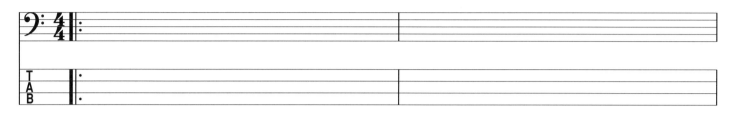

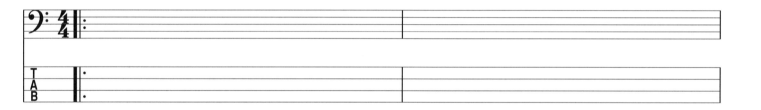

FIG. 6.8. Write Your Own Slap/Tapping Techniques

ETUDE: MR. JUNGLE

53: Full Band
54: Just Drums
55: No Bass

David Marvuglio

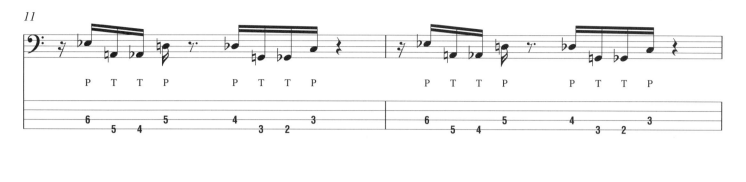

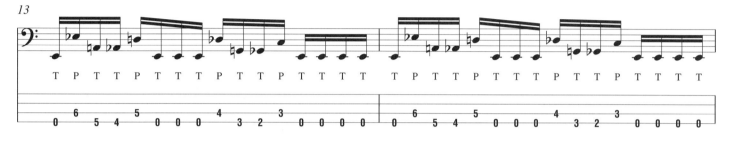

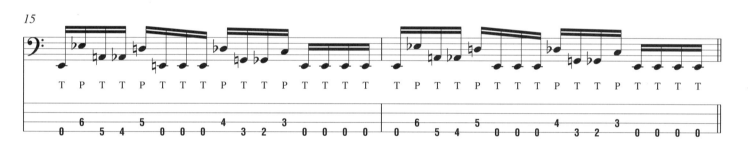

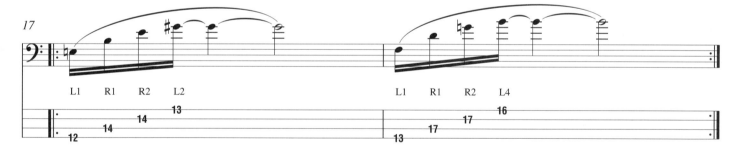

FIG. 6.9. Mr. Jungle

LESSON 7

Odd Meters

In modern metal, it is very common to play odd meters. This has been a natural step of the progression in the genre. Odd meters refer to grooves that are beyond duple and triple meters—usually combining them, such as 5 (3+2, 2+3), 7 (2+2+3, etc.), 11 (2+3+3+3, etc.), and beyond. The following exercises have different combinations of these groupings.

This 5/4 example can be subdivided with a pulse of 3+2 or 2+3. Accent the following groupings accordingly.

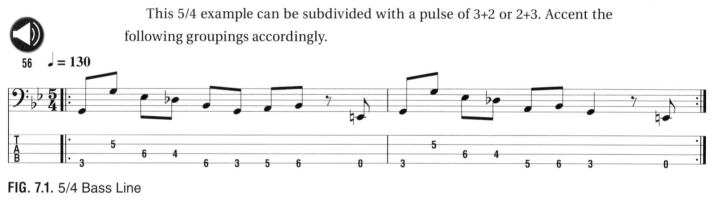

FIG. 7.1. 5/4 Bass Line

This next example is in 7/8, grouped 2+2+3.

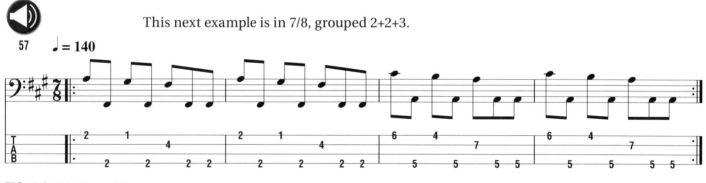

FIG. 7.2. 7/8 Bass Line

Here's an example in 11/8, with a 3+3+3+2 pulse.

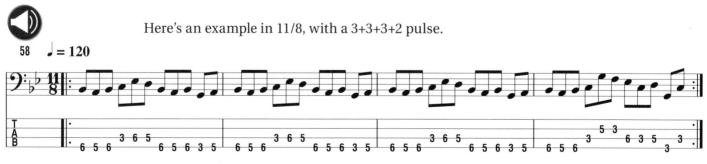

FIG. 7.3. 11/8 Bass Line

The following examples change meters. First, the time changes from 5/4 to 4/4. Try playing all these examples with different pulse groupings. For example, the 5/4 could be grouped as 3+2 or 2+3. The 4/4 measure could be grouped with the three eighth notes grouped together, or with four eighth-note figures together, or combining the two, with groups of three and then four eighths at the end of bar 3.

FIG. 7.4. 5/4 to 4/4

In this example, the pulse changes time from the quarter note to the eighth note. The 7/8 measure actually feels like 3½/4. Really, the eighth note remains constant through the whole example, as if the 4/4 was 8/8.

FIG. 7.5. 4/4 to 7/8

Here, we are playing a slap line using odd meters with a change of time. The quarter note is constant. Focus on emphasizing the 3/4 pulse and 4+3 pulse in the 7/4.

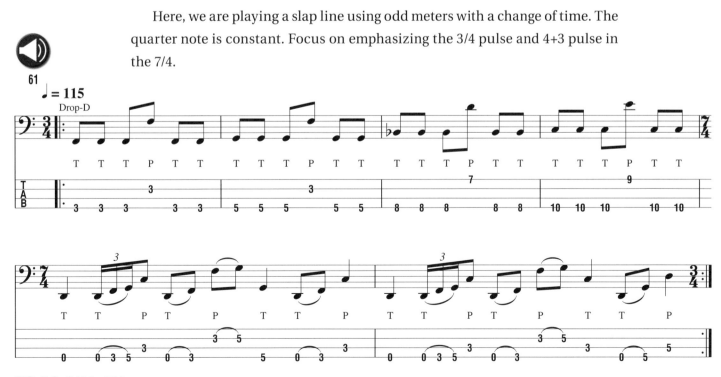

FIG. 7.6. 3/4 to 7/4

WRITE YOUR OWN

Write your own bass lines using odd meters and changing meters in the space below.

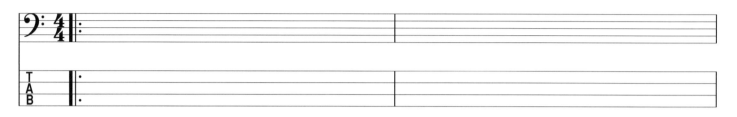

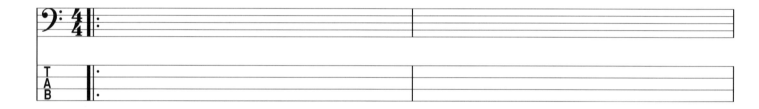

FIG. 7.7. Write Your Own Odd Meters

ETUDE: YEAH, I CAN COUNT THAT

62: Full Band
63: Just Drums
64: No Bass

David Marvuglio

FIG. 7.8. Yeah, I Can Count That

LESSON 8

Rhythmic Cycles

As an extension of odd meters, metal bands have progressed into superimposing odd metered rhythmic figures over different time signatures. In metal, this is uniquely referred to as a *rhythmic cycle*, and it has its origins in Indian music. In other genres, the technique is sometimes referred to as "*metric modulation.*"

A rhythmic cycle is created by repeating a syncopated rhythm riff so that it results in a feeling of one time signature over another. The effect is essentially a polyrhythm, such as 3 against 4, 5 against 4, or 7 against 4, depending on where the syncopations are placed.

The subdivisions we learned in the odd meters lesson apply to this technique, and we will really be paying attention to subdividing here as well. We will also discuss "the tail," which is a musical cue used to bring you back to the original time feel.

In this bass line, we are cycling a rhythmic duration of three sixteenth notes over 4/4.

65

♩ = 80

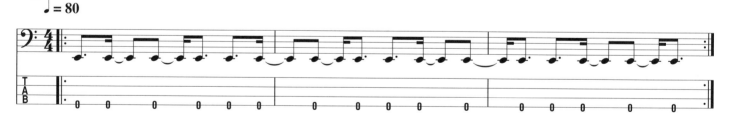

FIG. 8.1. Cycle of Three Sixteenths

Here we are cycling a grouping of five sixteenth notes over 4/4.

66

♩ = 80

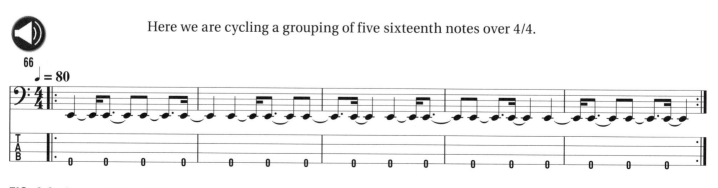

FIG. 8.2. Cycle of Five Sixteenths

Here, we are cycling a grouping of seven sixteenth notes over 4/4.

67 ♩ = 80

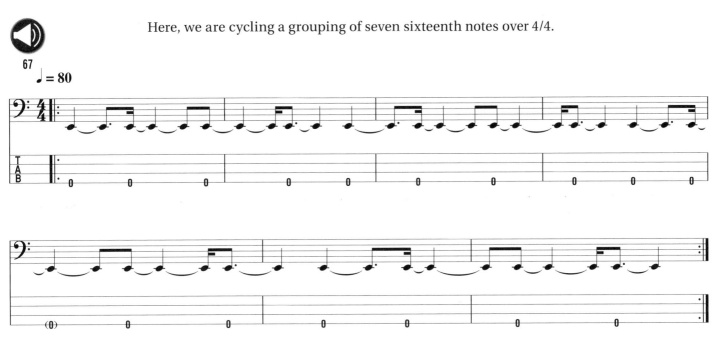

FIG. 8.3. Cycle of Seven Sixteenths

Here is a rhythmic cycle of three sixteenth notes with a tail to make it a four-bar phrase.

68 ♩ = 80

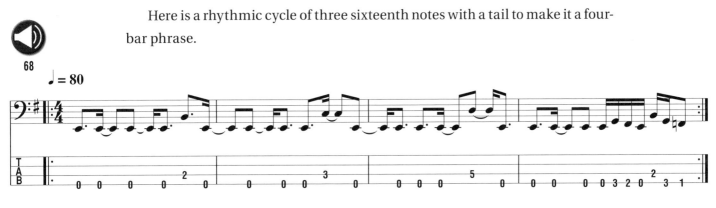

FIG. 8.4. Cycle of Three Sixteenths with Tail

Here is a rhythmic cycle of eighteen (grouped 5+5+5+3) sixteenth notes with a tail added at the end to make it a four-bar phrase.

69 ♩ = 90

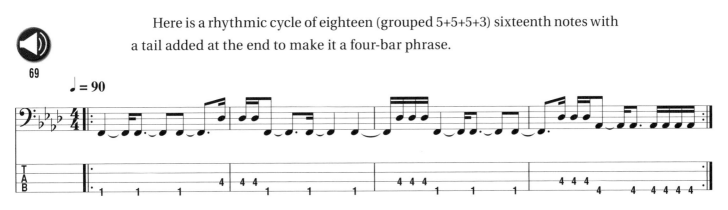

FIG. 8.5. Cycle of Eighteen Sixteenths with Tail

Here is a rhythmic cycle of 3+3+4 sixteenth notes with a tail added at the end to make it a two-bar phrase.

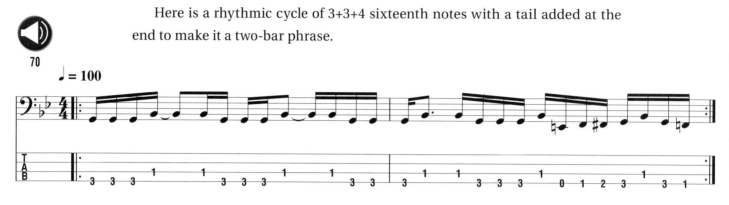

FIG. 8.6. 3+3+4 Cycle with Tail

WRITE YOUR OWN

Write your own bass lines using rhythmic cycles. Try composing some with a
tail to make four-bar phrases.

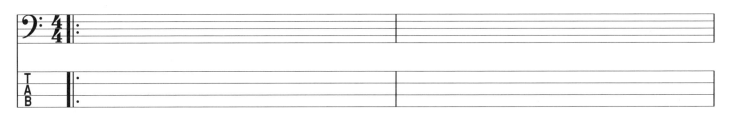

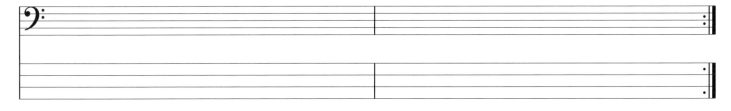

FIG. 8.7. Write Your Own Rhythmic Cycle

ETUDE: DON'T TELL ME...BLOODY NUMBERS

71: Full Band
72: Just Drums
73: No Bass

David Marvuglio

FIG. 8.8. Don't Tell Me...Bloody Numbers

ABOUT THE AUTHOR

Photo by Mia Olson

David Marvuglio teaches bass and ensembles at Berklee College of Music, where his *Metal Bass Lab* has been the inspiration for this book. David has appeared as a bass clinician at the Panama Jazz Fesitval and other international venues. He received the prestigious Uchida Fellowship where he studied traditional Japanese music with the intent to infuse this tradition into metal bass playing. David has toured with Ice Nine Kills, the Smyrk, and Emily Peal.